BIZARRE WINERY TRAGEDY

OTHER BOOKS BY THE AUTHOR

Ivanhoe Station
Full Magpie Dodge

BIZARRE WINERY TRAGEDY

Lyle Neff

ANVIL PRESS | VANCOUVER

Bizarre Winery Tragedy
Copyright © 2005 by Lyle Neff

All rights reserved. No part of this book may be reproduced by any means without the prior written permission of the publisher, with the exception of brief passages in reviews. Any request for photocopying or other reprographic copying of any part of this book must be directed in writing to ACCESS: The Canadian Copyright Licensing Agency, One Yonge Street, Suite 1900, Toronto, Ontario, Canada, M5E 1E5.

NATIONAL LIBRARY OF CANADA CATALOGUING IN PUBLICATION DATA
Neff, Lyle
Bizarre winery tragedy / Lyle Neff.

ISBN: 1-895636-66-3
I. Title
PS8577.E335B59 2005   C811'.54   C2005-901902-6

Printed and bound in Canada
Cover design: Rayola Graphic Design
Typesetting: HeimatHouse

Represented in Canada by the Literary Press Group
Distributed by the University of Toronto Press

The publisher gratefully acknowledges the financial assistance of the B.C. Arts Council, the Canada Council for the Arts, and the Book Publishing Industry Development Program (BPIDP) for their support of our publishing program.

Anvil Press
P.O. Box 3008, Main Post Office
Vancouver, B.C. V6B 3X5   CANADA
www.anvilpress.com

For Junie and James, at last

CONTENTS

- 9 Ground Floor
- 10 Jumper
- 11 Toronto Dominion Vision
- 12 How Did You Feel?
- 13 Powerpoint Presentation
- 14 Infancy
- 15 Fun Crisis
- 16 Sabbath Off Howe Street
- 17 That Moody Bastard
- 18 Halloweenthink
- 19 HMCS Unable, or Three Ways To Sink
- 20 Yaasriel's Seventy
- 21 Sitting Idly On The Banks Of The Fraser
- 23 Paraplegic City
- 24 Blind Camera
- 25 Mirror, Mirror
- 26 Lies I Am Heartily Sorry I Told, Yet Pleased They Were Believed
- 27 God Knows We're Not Suckers
- 28 Time Lapse
- 30 So What's The Latest?
- 31 Heather McTavish Does
- 32 Backyard Swelter
- 33 Letter To The Skyscrapers
- 34 "An Ague Hath My Ham"
- 35 Think Of Teeth
- 36 Gumboot Divorce

- 37 For J., After Waking Life
- 38 The Cure For Hatred
- 39 Change Table Dream
- 40 Among Women (Part Two)
- 41 Teenage Mob
- 42 Children Past Europe
- 43 Forget Your Cigarettes, Dagmar
- 44 Anyone With Experience Knows How To Put A Drunk In A Cab
- 45 "The Punctual Rape"
- 46 After Seeing Harris And Konstabaris
- 47 Eternal Laundromat
- 48 Clearihue Philosophy
- 49 Elizabeth II At Centre Ice
- 50 Dominion Day
- 51 Twenty Reasons To Go North
- 52 Burn The House To Ashes. Sow The Ashes With Salt. Never Go Back.
- 53 Mars
- 54 Crazy Sick Spare Change
- 55 Corrugated Woman
- 56 Karen's Finale
- 57 By Early July
- 58 Gathercole's Sudanese Possibilty
- 59 Doug's Quality of Life Improves When He Starts to Think of Celebrity as a Disease
- 60 Better Known Than Famous
- 61 Antihistamine

GROUND FLOOR

Right there in the climbing elevator she kissed
him, and their proposed three handsome kids
sang in a never-to-be choir, sang of
bad ideas, new ideas, the duty owed
to mouldering bouquets and disincentives,
slushed commutes and endless unanswered
cries in rooms of pitiless geometry;

The elevator rose and rose, she slid
a hand into his whispering shirts, her rings
ticked like a windowbound cat staring
out at starlings and vermin, his absence
at her funeral lumbered into shape
round their pitched figures, then
the fluorescents guttered, guttered

And glared back; ten digits fell slowly
past their still forms, the garbled overhead
intercom chanted of the thousand Sundays
they wouldn't know; but as if asleep
and cold she pressed the small back
of his back to her, uncalculated, failed
and he stepped into her, unsure of nothing

JUMPER

The train passed over the Scotch broom
and oil-stained clay of the last Vancouver
wasteland: human figures down in it
looked like handsome rain-cold pioneers,
surveyors of future homesteads:
at least to his glazed glazed
shellac vision they did. There was a rusty comma
in that vacant land, but he'd run out of attention

By then, she had rested her temple
on the train's window glass, at the choking
drain-end of a day of mutiny in the cubicles,
meetings with the high,
meetings with the low. She was thinking
her voice was too loud
when the overhead said,
"This is Skytrain Control, Skytrain Control"

The jumper'd landed part in mud, part on rocks,
the jumper reached for his several teeth
as roots and canals flowered in him,
his yellow spine widening like the
lawns of his childhood. He saw
the man and woman in the stalled train
above, he delayed them, they delayed him

TORONTO DOMINION VISION

I believed a jet-black daydream today,
Alone in the bank queue. Huge damp

Windows fogged the Square's light lawn,
Simple wants shuffled us along,

Spaced out—Then a vast crow dove steeply
Into the fountain, scattered the people and

Exploded in feathers of doom!

—No, it was a
Black truck raced by right then with a

Big stereo boom. Daydream luck, anyway!
I'll take hundreds, please, anyday.

HOW DID YOU FEEL?

Like a chaotic small terrorist
operation, was how she'd felt.

One faction was all fiery, fired up
with dynamite. They had briefly
got the upper hand and round

A shotglass went her fire-orange fingernails.
Couple of great leaders passed through
the bed. Then came to power the jittery faction,

With a jittery power, wrenched ideals,
drinking coffee. The sects in fact screeched
to and fro till they all blew up
in a work accident. Which explains,

She says, her hair and how brutally
she's aged. She thinks a man's life
is such an enviable ride.

"You should be an admiral, honey,"
she says, "a smoothie with no friction,
smart sailor of the prevailing tide."

POWERPOINT PRESENTATION

What speckled disaster I tossed down my gold
throat last night, fluidly commending freaks
to anomalous lives, though I don't know shit:

what a mean tiny apocalypse I'll be,
slapping cab hoods to turn out penniless neat
transvestites, cashless wigs in a black night:

still there's a labour lecture I'll never
get over. What foamed empty glasses right
here loom, while I speak in my old man's voice:

show me a daytime deadline, I must meet it.
Unrock fields, shovel shit, run the defenses;
this life, you work, the rest is pretense.

INFANCY

Baby's high-strung like winched-up wire,
navel and ass-rash and drilling whine
like ghosts are ripping at his diaper
to steal his flawless Baby soul; there;
Baby's ghosts are the ghosts of cats,
there, from the peat and branch medieval fires,

So Baby and I recline on the couch,
flannelled, buzzed and cried-out,
soft puppets onscreen;

I thought I had a principle,
it didn't survive the emergency,
so it wasn't a conviction ever,
it was just talk;

Baby doesn't know it,
grips my televisual finger.
There, Baby, Baby, Baby.

FUN CRISIS

How partial blurred faces might be
passed by an ambulance, I didn't see.
Was it the paramedic who sang along
among the latex gloves and red lights?
There was coughing enough to fill
even that siren-split evening,
I can promise you that

singing intertwined with it, exactly
as a blanket tangles stretcher'd legs.
It was a zoomy song amid the retching, too,
reverberant, restrained, precise, that voice!
As to the faces that must have sped by
beyond the latches, didn't see, dark glass.
But strings break at the height of glam'rous

sweaty-drunk rock shows, too, no one
is quite killed by it. Nor by IV poles
clanking on banked corners, nor by curses,
nor by reds run on a partial blurred night.

SABBATH OFF HOWE STREET

on weekend afternoons in commercial
space, the equipment needs to warm up

for the lines get clogged with messages
like winter wasps in a paper nest, and
the startled overheads take some waking

like me the lights are near-popping and frantic,
you can only force so much energy down
a thin skein before the wires dry out

and I can see my reflection above a divider,
a severed head bobbing towards a cheque

I've known women to bang shut the financial drawer
of must-do, overdue, get-to-now, then
turn to a finer thing, on a Sunday evening

THAT MOODY BASTARD

Likes to sit near beach statuary, is amiable,
has stubble like an old old man, sometimes
feels that what he's saying is repulsive
or that he's repulsed by what he's said.

Makes a violent gesture, a pigeon flock
naturally explodes just then. You could die,
laughing, poor guy in his pea coat
of despair, his ethical self-loathing,

How hard done by he's really been, how
he's barely survived. Let's give
the moody bastard a hi-test to celebrate
how low in the water the coal freighters run,

How the flock congregates again
around his cheap spotless half-laced runners.

HALLOWEENTHINK

High-hatted in pubs, masked with explosives—
St. Nick, let it be Halloween every day,
little cruelties allowed, big unstable crowds,
Burning Schoolhouses and painted heels
clocking each lane and curb, anti-yule
tide of revelry round firework'd
sedans, hey tumult, tumultuous sparks—
let the city's dogs cringe,

inside the plastic monsters dreams are condensing.
Dreams of tattered fields bent madly
under moonlight, dreams of snakes
kin molting like wrecked umbrellas there.
Let the stressed curs flee, All Hallows Eve's
thorny spree is in a steamed-up double-face,
night without mirrors, night of wet masks,
hellrazored, tricky feats, amen.

HMCS UNABLE, OR THREE WAYS TO SINK

First, majestically, with a wave from the deck,
one hopes, the floes cracking with
applause, seafloor as cold as irrelevance,
the cook drunk in the galley
with the scuppers and jags—

Or flailing miserably, not a gram of dignity,
like murderers' prey, knocking over
knick-knacks, stars shooting up
away from you through water,
for all your pleading hoarseness—

Or stoically, like a vine whose tree's cut,
whose leaves lie graceless on the ground,
diehard, prone as prone can be,
sunk and unable, but coiled and green,
never upright nor ever gone

YAASRIEL'S SEVENTY

I have the tapes of the dog-headed season
when ur-reason knelt hard by lust's broken doors;

The recording angel caught each facet
of those days, those days that snagged and prowled

Like static electricity down dirty handlebars; when
the crammed rooms got loud and snappy; when

A sonic boom rolled from eye to eye; it's all video'd,
conga backtracks sewn in, garbled shouts played

backwards, I have the tapes of the dog-headed season.
For the recording angel skulked then high atop

The eavestroughs, his sandalstraps tangled
the cable wire, with his baffles, sensors
and right ugly divinity garlanded about;
look the tapes can be got, the angel bought,

And the editors with their page rips and data clips
brought in divinely; look, the dog-headed season
can be housebroken for a time.

SITTING IDLY ON THE BANKS OF THE FRASER

Hell's Gate
Sit idly by the Fraser a few millenia,
and the body of your enemy will float by.

A little poochy-jowled, blue-skinned,
pocked by sturgeons—yeah, those

Bottom-monsters'll still swim even
then. But not your sightless rival,

Now called Bob, eddied, fatted,
that hated body floating by.
On the banks of the Fraser,

It's your long idleness that's key,
lounging tireless at the lodgepole tree

Two Streams
Film crews, log booms, fish markets,
strangled canyons, rich tourists,
delta pastures, Salish tribes.

Wide nets, bright billboards,
salmon ladders, sawdust heaps,
high bridges, Bombardier engines.

Ice floes, Fort George, Simon Fraser,
gold dust, fibreoptic cable, tugboats,
old waters, dead bodies, small houses.

Tributary
Teeth and water have got cold relations.
The old girl saw three forest fires take
two children and one drunken uncle,
the fireweed came later but so what,
its needy stalks humiliated her in '49.
Forced mouth-deep into Fraser muskeg
she saw those long blossoms explode again
in flame, she knows what a parasite is,
it's not the blaze but the dirty smoke,
so what. You can squeeze fluoride in
to corners; but only in the holes & hollows
of the jawbone will river water work.

PARAPLEGIC CITY

for Mike Tripp

I met the shorebirds, spoke poorly
to the gulls (all peevish squawking),
dreamed a straight drop to the cement,
wingless. Birds don't get this,

Crows don't have falling dreams,
they have walking dreams.
So we talk to these creatures,
chickadees starlings and such airy

scraps whose names I dunno. Pigeons
you know, their big-street struts, cooing
like fast-busy tones on a phone, how

they clutch wires at sunset, pause,
ready to launch up like townbirds—
I fell straight on cement, dreamed
of walking, met the shorebirds

BLIND CAMERA

You can't see it coming. How cement breaks up
As roots bust its back, all through your childhood years.

You can't see bright days coming, nor all the accidents,
Nor blacknesses that make flares into shadows.

Though you can hear the gunpowder hiss in flares,
Penumbra of sibilant points mapped around you.

Navigating, navigator. Navigator, rise up
And be strong: blindnesses ending, work to be done.

MIRROR, MIRROR

So here's what I live with, me. Look
at his gesticulative tics and what
a poor clued-out cock-knocker
he is, one boot in the gutter,
the fullness of totems
and national tattoos round
his full furred belly, all creak
and squawk about something,
baby. I don't mind his rotten
breath and how he jolts awake,
not so much. He's not too bad a guy,
stacks three doubled pillows
under his fat head, brackets
his Missus in a curve,
likes a tin of tuna with mayo
on white bread, stays loyal
to his abysmal team, paws
around at knowable things,
pauses mumbling by dawn
gas stations like any newcomer,
alone, harsh-clothed, chattering

LIES I AM HEARTILY SORRY I TOLD, YET PLEASED THEY WERE BELIEVED

1. That J. had sculpted a nativity scene out of ham
2. That young MacD. weighed 9 kilos at birth
3. That the blazer was due to my court appearance for assault
4. That I was a French-Montrealais named Dieppe
5. That I read the whole thing
6. That the softball team subjected T. to a brutal hazing ritual involving piss-toast
7. That the Minister had sold the Ontario lakefront to an American consortium
8. That an "IPO" was a kind of paperwork for whores
9. That I was a lawyer for well-connected gangsters
10. That I was briefly 6'4"

GOD KNOWS WE'RE NOT SUCKERS

But winter's attenuation is busting some chops today,
shapely mould legs flex down the flanks
of cladded condos. Blue tarps flip in the wind,
throwing off a bit of rainwater like a light sweat.

It's not just that winter's insinuation crawls
everywhere, but also the water's so leaden cold,
And there has been a shoddy sporous era.
This is winter's application to old Granville town:

A hole cold as lawsuits, as grim to struggle out of.
Can movie stars tank-topped on Robson
erase the theft of so many homes? We stand
but so much of Vancouver's gone down
without a crack or rumble, just leaned down
and subsided damply, in a heavy rotten wind.

TIME LAPSE

In the flap of a shutter she's running
in the wind, my greasy army jacket
snaps lithely along her skinny wrists,
the photo smells good, good, good.
Unlike the walls of that hard school
falling on my exciteable head,
she doesn't close in; she's a crow
on a snowy powerline, her time
has ascended, she skips out of girlhood
through ankle-deep powder, click.

She's been having impertinent spikes
of holy feeling on a European Grand Tour,
had it off in hostels on the Thames, huge
backpack lolling from a freckled shoulder,
in the shot she's strong, strong
as the gulls skimming the brine.
Entwined and numbly young at home,
dumb for redheads, I'm filing postcards,

Snap. Snap of an unashamed ivory woman
with a leering great pregnant belly
in a fig-treed backyard, that squint
she always has, asking the camera,

how do you like looking on me,
am I the image you've just got to see?
Film will emulsify; oxygen in the end
makes it die; but she's like the starling,
etched everywhere in this history—
the eye changes, not what it sees.

SO WHAT'S THE LATEST?

Nearly nothing, I go about talking,
Bending fires and putting out ears, same old
Slow mould, putting the security scars up
To the feeder, dazing in the elevator;

Watching a designer carstrap her infant
Then plunk the glove compartment shut
As the fluorescents gutter, flicker, gutter
And flood up; I only stand and doze,

Watching feebly as usual, poking the remote,
Dressing on least-filthy principles; friend,
I've been round yakkin' like before and since,
Since life either enjoys me, or I like it.

HEATHER MCTAVISH DOES

Put her little black Chevy in the handicapped
spot. "I'm handicapped by being drunk,
yeah?" Good as words the bad girl hip-bumps
the parking meter and beer-store doorframe,
throwing off corrupt glitter powder—damn, Heather!—
in every collusion of her days-long nights.

I wear mitts, I do rails at
the glove compartment, I sing a bit
of black and grey streaks in the blonde world,
flashlights on lost lines of powdered fun,
but something in me whinnies with fear.

Yeah: a high-pitched deafening
whinny, as emitted by horses and fools,
timorous in the passenger seat of Heather's run.

BACKYARD SWELTER

Your interest gets caught
like a trout on a double-barb,
tugged in with a lot of splashing;

Your whole attentive attention
leans in, its many fingers reach.
Paradoxically,

You set down the drink now,
sit back laconically, let
comrades of the ancien regime

Do their worthwhile talking. Old friends
who know from back in the day,
anyone who's seen you lose,

That's who you listen to.

LETTER TO THE SKYSCRAPERS

You dwarf nothing, I feel a shabby grin-faced
Exuberance among your grey flanks

Anyway, and in the mountains I miss you.
Can't you leave me alone, with your weight

And vulnerabilty? Towers, I'm slave to your
Windowed constellations: the Party,

The Television Family, the Lonely
One. I love your star charts of backlit lives,

But you don't love me back, my built creatures,
Buttressed, wired, piped, designed, maintained

Creatures. You'll live forever, unless a tremor
Knocks you down. Keep scraping the sky, I ask you.

"AN AGUE HATH MY HAM"

A word like "ague" is like a man
who travels all over the place,
means different things at different ages,
then goes entirely out of use.
Of course all men are like that;
of course all words are like that; but

Our descendants won't get even this,
our talk'll be fuckin' "thee" and "thou"
to them, 1000 years post-them our
fine thoughts'll not be as useful
as gob on the sidewalk, and it's painful.
Still I'd plump for "an ague hath my ham,"

Since sure as taxes, there'll still be men
who'll still have asses, and irrational hassles
afflicting them. Even the Old Testament
says there will always be assholes.
"An ague," 34th-century man will say,
"An ague hath my ham."

THINK OF TEETH

I'm asking you to think of teeth, I can't be made
to think on teeth this plaqued and bent-grown
day, this bitten-over and de-enamelled
day, with its damp manta of a thought
lolling about beneath, hinged in its
ridged troughs underneath—

Christ! Christ. Turn the radio higher,
I said higher, I can't get the right kinda
signal, can't pick up its force,
though the antenna's rooted so
high in the skull, it's
slickly conductive—

You've never seen the teeth in your mouth,
you've just seen images.

                        I can't think how
to ask you for your thought of teeth,
I can't think of them anymore, I may
never think again.

                Of teeth anyway,
though the day we don't think anything—
that day's coming, cuts right through.

GUMBOOT DIVORCE

Flies on a near-dead moose, baby.
Bottle-blue proof a half-dead thing's
got to be daggered gently down,
not blunt-instrumented. Sassy glossed
flies haven't even got teeth.
Still they'll get every scrap till it's gone.

Hazelton's wife crossed the parking lot alone,
violent turns in her big hips, whole town
watched that churning Hazelton's wife walk,
even her hair blew straight out behind her.

There was a route to happiness, her
clan saw later, but much to break down
first. You're trying to kill someone,
and you just inject eggs into his head?
And all those scrappy laden carapaces,
the flies, buzzed, bathed in Northern dusk,
lowly across the lilies of Beloved Lake.

FOR J., AFTER WAKING LIFE

So we dream, so what? Likely it's gibberish,
you fly the downtown canyons
or your leg's a kilometre long. But hey what
a shiver as your bootheels levitate. The sweat
on that weak city-sized leg. That's real.
Dreams are the realest nonsense; realer,

And the forlorn engine of consciousness
never gets shut off, never is cleaned.
No wonder we wake woven with pain
that fades while we stare wandering
over coffee and orange slices on a plate; we
must lie back down; it's all the same dream.

THE CURE FOR HATRED

There's no cure. But a sweet way to snuff
out anger is to hunt for cardboard boxes
on a drizzly day in the lanes with
a baby reaching up her fat arms.

Yeah, she likes the dogs and
the corroded carports and has
no knowledge but us. You can see
a lot worse in her way,
some degraded furniture,
peculiar oils and plaids.

When you find the fuckin' boxes,
it feels insane you ever sought 'em.
And the child's got no grievance,
to her a sheaf of stainy cardboard is
the damp wall of the cure, or just as good.

CHANGE TABLE DREAM

Me and our son stirring up the mud,
baying like trapped dogs in the cold swamp;
I hold the tiny man up like a megaphone,
his batteries short-popped and circuiting—
my son's muddy cries, my muddled eyes,
the quicksand round my yap quickening—

Then you slosh in on the propellorboat, darling;
take hold of his fat elbows and mud-caked
ribcage, lift him with a pock! sound into
your savecraft, while your swampship stereo
plays crackedly: the world is a vampire,
the world is a vampire;

And then you elbow me and give MacDuff me,
slatted sun rising across we three;
I'll change the stare-baby and bring him back,
brush foul dreams like burrs off my bathrobe;
I'm in the oddest love, come away O human child

AMONG WOMEN (PART TWO)

Among women at weddings there's a huddling factor,
a look over bare shoulders maybe, a muscle

Tautened thin below the hem, laughter in heels,
arrangements arrived at in bathroom stalls. So

Maybe the moon will spread butter on your jaw
or some females swoon onto the banquet; so

Let every tired bird flutter down. Be the stoic goon
fireworks bounce off of, be the calm women think of.

TEENAGE MOB

Unrehearsed, altogether a sad case, people are
infected hearts, ebullience, broken arms. C'mon,
we're just kids. Bubbly, busted, moons many
in the sky and out of passing trucks. Can't
enjoy that? Take this bottle, take the stick

Out of your ass. Every story has three sides, we're
young, so a sparkler bomb's designed on cement,
set off in the bush.

We'll go completely nuts when it goes up,
that friendly hiss and chaotic pop.
It is so loud and quiet wherever we are.

CHILDREN PAST EUROPE

God's man came down in principle and a comic hat,
A jumble of gravel leaked from his sorry arms.
Later, money-changers lurked around back:
Myrrh and olive oil and Samaritan girls to be had.

Here I'm bathing my girl in a godless cold
Canadian lake, leeches gasping away from
Cheap shampoo, her giggled terror,
Near to lilies and overhung drenched poplars.

She never saw a desert. Never will be a desert.
She's the tribalist of freshwater glacier gravel
And trout chasing, a thin-towel cape changer
Who forces bears back in a wingbone shiver.

FORGET YOUR CIGARETTES, DAGMAR

No graceful exit goes unmarred
by your coarse impromptu return. It's truest
in crisis-fired, quit-or-be-sacked season, now-
or-never-breakup time; for some poison reason

You leave your wallet behind in every war room.
The injured party, you crack doors lately slammed,
scuttle in for keys, coats, stuff; pretty shook up,
but proud, like a prison visitor—such crap theatre!

Check yourself before every door, enemy. Get a good go,
Tap each pocket and principle. Make your going gone.

ANYONE WITH EXPERIENCE KNOWS
HOW TO PUT A DRUNK IN A CAB

Or so I said hotly. Before I got suspicious and sick
Of myself, suddenly. What a capacious sink I'd need
to hold my life's dirty water.

We'd been getting high
for hours, there'd been much to roar & roam
through.

But through, we were all just about through.
A curtain of zigzag bolts & silence was descending,
& it was deafening.

"THE PUNCTUAL RAPE"

In fact you wake sick with glad-
ness daily, since nuthin fires up a numb
head or useless guilt like a ring-
ing phone or postie on the steps,
christ, not quite. All that fighting pricey
gassy talk at the pub swats at your
woken mind—now you've got to earn the price
of conscience again, and again
think of what you claimed last night,
your debunkings debunked and wit
stripped dumb. Good to have work innit?

AFTER SEEING HARRIS AND KONSTABARIS

The afternoon rebrightened,
it had been a grim grey one. Robin
went by preoccupied, Reed told me
part of his divorce as he caught the 20,
I was on the corner to have a smoke,
it was six or so and raining. Carefully
my son MacD. in feety pajamas
two storeys above walked along the coffee table.

Did you know, citizens Konstabaris and Harris,
and determined neighbours of 4th and Commercial
who erect storefronts in the rain,
you widened the future again?

ETERNAL LAUNDROMAT

When I've got a revulsion I try to end it,
Or nurture it to death anyway. O anger,
O pretty blushing little chancre,
to be petted and to mewl, sinking
your spindly root-veins deeper in;
O much-carried grudge,
let me hunch across the crosswalk
in seconds for scab-faced once.

Now I despise my hatings,
I need to escape that foamy loathing,
you know how it is, Christ.
That little rinse cycle of roundabout hate.
Matchbooks in the dryer for 40 minutes.
And feeling better later.

CLEARIHUE PHILOSOPHY

She said, "You can only see and hear
what you can see and hear. And
that's a shadow of the real world."

She stood by her desk and
looked way tall to me, till
the section of floor my desk
stood on started to sink. I mean,

A shadow? That papery oddment
pinned to your heels, that black
water the moon wobbles through?
That's a cartoon of the world,
it's not even close . . . you have got
to make maps, and infer and guess
off the shadow. Amazing
when you think about it.

Amazing even when you don't. I looked hard
at the philosopher, wondered what else she
might invisibly be, wondered aloud
at her shadowy height

ELIZABETH II AT CENTRE ICE

History hauled off its gory boots here,
History swore off its roving mobs. Just
A taxi now glitters over the Cambie span,
Paced with yellow flickering on Pacific wave-
Lets. AM radio ticks in the cab, AM radio
As good as silence. You can use the armrest,
Free of anxiety, free as freedom gets.

History hit the mattress hard here,
History crossed out no lists of names.
One last hate-filled woman lives by the Drive,
And when she kicks through cherry drifts
She laughs so hard her eye gets wet.
Once she was stabbed and stabbed,
She's alive, alive as you can get.

DOMINION DAY

Canada's as free and strong as she's called,
and way more beautiful. Even her
shuffling packs of lawyers catch something
of her, in the strings of their unravell'd cuffs;
How there's a metal tin of bandages on a shelf
by an ashtray in the Northwest Territories,
while everyone's out on the long lake;
That Canada's lost sons carp in the editorial
pages, prescribing from abroad—hey, d'you miss
something? A raft on a lake, not even drifting . . .
Maybe we miss *them*. In a meeting you take
your smokes, papers, keys, throw everything
on the table. We're mostly durable, in love with work
of the worthwhile sort, the strong and free kind.

TWENTY REASONS TO GO NORTH

the radical Southernness
of life down here.
the failure of appointments.
the stood-up standoff,
the no-show, the blow-off,
the bloodless lose-it.
the permanent not-knowing-if.
the studied rudeness of
the it band that blows.
the chatterbox ranting
of the badass bus driver,
the desperate state
of the Number Eight's
endless debate
on meetups missed,
changes of plans,
so-influential friends.
the pounders of pavement,
dreams of government,
of the pockmarks all on all:
gimme a little town, a big mountain.

BURN THE HOUSE TO ASHES. SOW THE ASHES WITH SALT. NEVER GO BACK.

There's not a pretty estrangement
in this world. Relations do get severed,
thank Christ, thank Christ . . . and the dead
boots in the closet can just stay dead there.

We weren't made as disjointed as we are
for just slotting in, one as one, two by two.
*I don't wanna touch you, I don't wanna
kiss you.* Stars aren't the moon, the manna
went venomous. You took your things and slouched
out, irradiated.

So go draw your words in dust on
the trunk of a Chevy. There's no pretty
estrangement, do you remember? I'd forgot.
There's a pleasure in not knowing you.
And your knowing me has already stopped.

MARS

Here's kids under the astronomical second,
all lanky boys with telescopes under Mars's approach;
Touching and trying all tall pimply girls; what grief
and anger, what lenses among the observant brats.
Mars is a war planet just 60 million clicks away,
a war planet where you can hold a hand or two,
an astronomical second or two.

CRAZY SICK SPARE CHANGE

O night's jacket is on your nightish shoulders,
you spavined vigilante of the number 20
stop—you who buttons up a little, puts a transfer
into the reader wrongly, and backs down squeaking—
listen, beggar: beer-and-wines close at 11 and only take
5 doz of clean tins. Chinese grandmothers raze Vancouver's
recycleable-tetrapak market, their suffering
trumps yours. Or does it. Or does it suffer,
the East End moonlight carefully painted
on all miners, we aluminum-siding psychics
at the bottle depot. Some isolates, some hermits.
Some from towns built by Alcan, wood and Victoria.
Does the moonlight get awfully wounded
in the jacket of a Lower Mainland night.

CORRUGATED WOMAN

I'll tell you the saga of the corrugated woman.
Remember this: her nature is rollercoasterish,
she rises and falls, shallow valleys, high peaks.
Corduroy woman exists in long straight lines too,
parallel to the walking spirit, the upright thing.

She walked straight today over many snake-pits,
plus an hour's journey each way. Linear woman
had that buzz of sweat at the hairline when she
got in at 7. A bowl of food, books, a sleep
on the cushion. I came in on a beam or two

of midnight moonlight, to touch her pale graphed
cheek. I see how womanhood's latitude, long
bell curves on a wavering grid, is the source
after all. No picture can show what there is in women,
can it? Uncapturable, their view of the borders of life.

KAREN'S FINALE

Every switch snapped off eventually
all round her deathbed and deathroom. Then
someone had to propose sandwiches and coffee

While that same mountain she'd lived
under for decades put its shade
on her waxen face. My hollowed sweet mother

I kissed her terrified. The king hummingbird
showed his ruby throat later at her feeder
on the deck. It was that Wiser's whisky

Held in our misery I think or the Bulkley River
at that 5 acres on the bend where
we sweated and talked her out.

BY EARLY JULY

It's to be a summer of funerals apparently.
The heat and the pressure driven so high up,

The highway's wavering. The driveway crunches
as dozens of trucks pull to a stop, mourners

in blazers step down with casseroles and whisky,
mosquitoes already tormenting them, while

A soldierly row of fireweed bows in curt unison.
Later the deaths dissipate and the orations try to halt

GATHERCOLE'S SUDANESE POSSIBILITY

I grew up on the strawberry-tinted slurry
that oils a chainsaw up
and makes the chain cry and bite.
I grew up on pucks whomped off boards,
CN trains over chasms,
chained tires on the crushed snow,
busted wild clans,
and so did you, pretty;

Except that you grew up in some
plane of sand, or at least the God-haunted
wastelands where you drove
your jeep full of rifles for the Egyptian Army.
I grew up there too, tho I know nothing
about it. And I saw you in the shadows
Friday at the reservoir party, when
it hit minus a few degrees,
you saw me brightly too.

DOUG'S QUALITY OF LIFE IMPROVES WHEN HE STARTS TO THINK OF CELEBRITY AS A NASTY DISEASE

He sees smudgy crows attack a parking-lot
snowbank, and in one sundered second
a kind of Arctic entirely seizes him;

He protests the avalache, will not
wear a "wool cap" so low over his eyes,
resists all Parliament and Dominion;

And is least seen raging through Gastown,
stealing coin from buskers and cursing
en francais, so tall and hard done by;

Banned from his theatres and encyclicals,
he's continuously shushed, ignores the source
of the ghostly streets around him, needs a pint

BETTER KNOWN THAN FAMOUS

Is anything more skeletally rumourous or half-
glimpsed than Reputation, is anything so ruinous,
I ask myself? I dunno,

I stand asking myself questions and handsignal
one more jug for the lot, I'm kinda on the spot.

Who knows what others really think?
Who knows? You? You can't even play Celebs,

I'm thinking, can't play Stars Movie Careers,
numb as I'm getting in the mouth and ears,

Can't we kill off these questions? Another toke,
I'll see bad motives in these friendly jokes,

And I'll think, how'm I thought of?, how
'm I thought of? (static broadcast), hey

Now let me unleash *my* bad opinion

ANTIHISTAMINE

Never used to get so sick so often.
This grey stubble in patches is also new.
Baby puts his arms round my neck now,
scrambles up me,
anxious about the belly-high sea, my
pale scrabbly ant, handsome as the foamy surf.

The harder his white arms clutch,
the wider death gets. It flies scythely
widescreen at us. I'm not ageless, and
someday he'll die too, I'm revolted by his

death loitering here; I lift him; you can't have him,
it's repulsive. You too were a child once
and still death'll kill you,

I was a child once and shall still get
killed by death, the last trustworthy day
was what? Generations ago?

ABOUT THE AUTHOR

Lyle Neff is a poet and literary journalist whose work has appeared in *The Vancouver Sun, Terminal City, subTerrain, Geist, The Westender,* and *The Georgia Straight*. His first collection of poetry, *Ivanhoe Station*, was a finalist for the Dorothy Livesay Poetry Prize in 1998. His second book of poetry was *Full Magpie Dodge* (Anvil). Born in Prince George in 1969, Neff lives in Vancouver with his wife and son.

OTHER ANVIL PRESS POETRY TITLES

Bogman's Music / Armstrong / $13.95
Full Magpie Dodge / Neff / $13.95
Honeymoon in Berlin / Walmsley / $16
Intensive Care / Twigg / $14
Ivanhoe Station / Neff / $10.95
Lonesome Monsters / Osborn / $10.95
Rattlesnake Plantain / Greco / $14
Sideways / Haley / $14
Singer, An Elegy / Fetherling / $14
Siren Tattoo / Greco, Mori, McIntyre / $10.95
Snatch / MacInnes / $12.95
Swing in the Hollow / Knighton / $13.95
Under the Abdominal Wall / McCartney / $11.95
Unravel / Armstrong / $16
Viral Suite / Rowley / $16
Where Words Like Monarchs Fly / McWhirter / $14.95

Write us for a free catalogue of books.

ANVIL PRESS PUBLISHERS
PO BOX 3008, MPO
VANCOUVER, BC
V6B 3X5
WWW.ANVILPRESS.COM